DEDICATED TO MY MOM & DAD,

WHO MADE ALL

OF THIS POSSIBLE.

Disclaimer:

Just to let you know, this book was made without any self-pity.

Feel free to laugh about my circumstances!

Rough Beginnings

So, like all stories (or diaries), I'll start from the beginning. In 2008, I got sick. I got meningitis to be exact, right before my sister was born. In fact, she was born the DAY I got out of the hospital. So that pretty much screams, "INTENSE!"

I had to have a magnet surgically placed on the surface of my skull and a cochlear implant (CI) put in my head, and I was fitted for a hearing aid in the other ear because I lost most of my hearing. I had other surgeries, too. Those were just the highlights. But on the bright side, I got to see Dallas in a helicopter while traveling to the hospital!

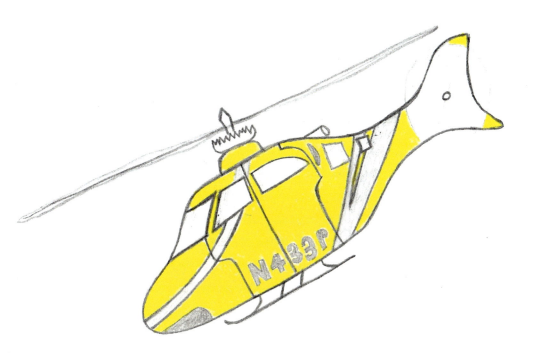

I Can't Hear You!

I am sorry to say that there have been times when I just didn't like my ears. Like when I was two, for instance, I used to hide my ears in the laundry basket.

Sometimes I used them to my advantage, for instance when I was little, whenever my mom would tell me to do something, I would flick off my ear and just walk past her. Boy, did that make her mad! Whenever kids would pick on me at school or just be annoying in general, I would turn the ears off, too.

But sometimes, although unintentionally, I would lose them. Like when I flushed my ear down the toilet a few years back and never re-trieved it (more on that later).

At the school Cafeteria...

Youth Group Hysteria

So, I was at my youth group playing throw-the-ball-at-everyone-show-no-mercy ...and... well, I definitely **got** my **share of** "lack-of-mercy"! Twice. Right on my cochlear implant. It broke, so I couldn't put it back on. Unfortunately, we played a fast game of get-to-know-you right after my CI broke. Like I said, I couldn't hear, so when I went up to say the guy's name, I said, "Nate." I was a little off. It was Daniel. I also embarrassed myself by misinterpreting a lot of other stuff. But of course, I'm gonna have to get used to that.

Ten-Grand-Down-the-Toilet

So, I'll bet you're dying to hear about my ear down-the-toilet story in detail. So, I'll tell you. It was just a normal day, and I was sitting on the toilet, minding my own business (get it?). But when I got up, my CI fell in the toilet... and I flushed!!! I just stood there for a few minutes in shock. Then, I ran all the way to my Mom's room. She was on the phone, talking to one of her business partners, and she must've seen how pale I was, so she asked me what was wrong. After I told her, she tried to do something with the toilet, like, to throw it back up or something. Then, since my Dad worked for the City, he asked the sewer treatment plant workers to retrieve it. To this day, that cochlear implant is but a distant memory.

I Become Mute

One day, I was at the park. It was just a normal day, with just a few little kids running around. Then suddenly, one of the kids walked up to me and asked, "Can you talk?" *What kind of a question is that?* I thought to myself. *What kind of person could be so inhumane to ask such a question?* Considering if the answer was, "No," there was probably no way they could receive the answer besides a headshake! *He's just a kid,* I reminded myself. So, I looked down at him and said, "No, I cannot talk," and walked away with a smirk.

I Deny the Knowledge
of My Own Name

One day, I was at the Civic Center for the All Region Band Rehearsal. I was playing trumpet (and still do), and I was second chair next to a guy named Hunter. Then, out of the blue, my nose started running like a water fountain, and I didn't get a break for two hours!! As if that wasn't enough, my CI died while I was playing! Hunter leaned over to ask me a question. I didn't want to look dumb by saying, "What?" a million times, so I just said, "I don't know." I wish I hadn't because he had said, "What's your name?"

Bionic Man

There were also times where I felt proud of my ability. Once my soccer coach asked me if I was in the secret service. Another time, I was at a gymnastics party, and the owner told me I was like a Bionic Man! I thought that was cool! When I was about seven or so, my mom had recently told me how to deal with people who asked questions. So, when a little girl walked up to me at the park and asked, "What's that on your head?" I replied with the usual, "It helps me hear." Then she said, "Cool! I wish I had one!"

Laundry Basket

Recently, I was at soccer practice playing a scrimmage when my hearing aid died. I still had my CI on, so I could hear. I put my ear inside of my bike helmet (I am within biking distance from my home), and I kept on playing. When practice was over, I rode off. I got in the shower and went to bed as usual. The next day, I went to my ear charger and saw something that made me go pale. Or maybe it was what I didn't see. I was humming a song at the time and BOY, did it shut me up! My hearing aid wasn't there!! My first thought was, *Really, Isaiah? You couldn't keep it for at least one year?* (It was practically new) I told my mom, and we went to the park to look for it. Even if all that was left of the hearing aid was a grease spot (Ok, maybe not a grease spot), you could send it to the hearing aid company as evidence to get a new one.

I went home to change, and you won't believe what I saw in the laundry basket! I had put it in my pocket after the practice and forgot to take it out after my shower. And the thing was, my mom did the laundry every morning and just forgot to that time. Thank God!

Luke Adams

A few years ago, Jimmy Joe (a family friend) arranged a day for a college basketball player named Luke Adams to meet me since he had two cochlear implants.

When I saw him, I was psyched! I wore a huge grin the entire time, not believing I was with a Texas Tech basketball player actually shooting hoops. Back then, I wasn't really deep with thought. I was just like, *Oh you have CI's too? Cool! Let's play Basketball!* But what really surprised me is what he gave me at the end. A **new, autographed, official, Texas Tech sweat** band! I was seven at the time, so you could imagine me treating the accessory with pride, as you would a priceless artifact.

Coolest Thing Ever

I used to watch videos on phones with my earphones, but I had the volume up so high that other people could hear the video clearly, like, word for word! It wasn't until a couple of weeks later when I realized that I might as well watch the video without earphones. So when my mom and I went to the Audiologist, I told him about how I liked my music and videos loud, while other people didn't. So he told me about this cord you could plug into your CI and the phone and no one around me would hear a thing! I have to admit, it is the coolest thing ever!

Minecraft

One time, I complained to my mom that the sounds coming into my CI were too loud. So she looked in the cochlear box in her closet and found this controller that could change the volume of sound that you hear. Well, she made the mistake of describing it with the word "phone," so I freaked with excitement! I asked her if I could play games on it or listen to music. So you can imagine how disappointed I was when I tried to play Minecraft.

My Disabilities
Become My Abilities

Luckily, my parents are really encouraging because if they were not, God knows what self-esteem level I would have! Probably 3 out of 100! Of course people still stare, ask stupid questions and stuff like that, but besides that, I am not really picked on. When I first started school, I was usually chosen last for P.E. games, but now people know that my disability doesn't change who I really am. And it makes my talents all the more unbelievable. Not to brag or anything, but for my age, I'm pretty good at the piano! Add that on top of the fact that I'm legally deaf, and it shows just how awesome God is!

RECO

TICKLIN' THE IVORIES

ISAIAH BAIER
Pickleman,©2018 KNICKNAK MEDIA

Playing background music without being able to hear the piano over all the talking...

This is what happens when you guess questions for the sake of your reputation... DO NOT Attempt!!!

Most Encouraging Letter Ever

In August of 2017, one of our friends, Todd, wrote me an amazing letter!

He told me to, "Always remember where your talent comes from [and] never apologize for what God has made you good at. If it doesn't matter to you, it doesn't matter to anyone else. ... You are gifted by God."

It was a very touching letter, and uh, he has only one real eye! So, he has every reason to feel sorry for himself, but he doesn't. That's the way we should all be.

Endangered, Closed Captions

Another funny thing: I can't understand songs or movies. I thought that this one song said, "radio cell," but it really said, "ready yourselves." I thought another song said, "You take the orphan's hair," but it really said, "You take the orphan's hand." I can't understand movies at all. So I REALLY need subtitles. Unfortunately, that makes the other viewers mad because it, like, covers up too much of the screen or something! I was watching this show with a little kid, and when I put subtitles on, he literally told on me!

How One Burger Saved My Life

I LOVE HAMBURGERS, and I'll tell you why. I was in the hospital, recovering from meningitis and laying in the crib, staring into space. I was only 21 months old, and I wasn't talking to anybody, and I wouldn't eat anything. Everyone was really worried as you can imagine! A few days later, my grandad, "Dado" (he wanted to be called Daddy-o" but you know, pronunciation of a two-year-old) walked in with a burger. I turned to look at him and stared at him while he ate. He came up to me showing me the hamburger to see if I would want a bite. I opened my mouth and took a HUGE chunk out of the thing, and I was better after that! Like I say now, "If it wasn't for that burger, I probably wouldn't be here right now." Of course, that's only partially true. Here is a picture of me in speech therapy learning how to pronounce my favorite word.

Good, Good Father

I was at my youth group one evening, and our band played a song for us. It was the song, "Good, Good Father." As it played, I realized that even though I had to go through a lot, God still enabled me to be able to play piano, trumpet, soccer, and write a book. The doctors did not expect me to live, and if I did, they did not expect me to walk or talk! I realize that God really is good.

Epilogue

For any of you who have cochlear implants or hearing aids, they are NOT burdens. They make you no different from anyone else. Don't be ashamed of them, and most importantly, don't let them limit you. You can be a doctor, a lawyer, a musician, a basketball player... anything!

What he said:

What I heard:

Made in the USA
Coppell, TX
25 August 2021

60932974R00024